Introduction

In today's fast-paced and demanding world, mental toughness and discipline have become increasingly crucial for success in all aspects of life. These traits enable individuals to persevere through challenges, maintain focus, and ultimately achieve their goals. The importance of cultivating mental strength cannot be overstated, as it serves as the foundation upon which personal and professional growth can occur.

The 75 Day Challenge Program is a transformative experience designed to help individuals develop mental toughness and discipline through a series of daily activities and practices. By committing to this program, participants can expect to see significant improvements in their physical, mental, and emotional well-being, as well as a renewed sense of purpose and motivation.

At the core of the 75 Day Challenge Program is the belief that personal transformation is achievable for anyone willing to put in the effort and dedication required. This journey is not about quick fixes or temporary solutions; it's about fostering lasting change and developing habits that will serve as the foundation for long-term success. By setting the stage for personal transformation, participants can embark on a journey of self-discovery and growth, ultimately unlocking their full potential.

A key component of the 75 Day Challenge Program is establishing clear, achievable goals and making a commitment to see them through. Goal setting is an essential aspect of personal growth, providing direction and a sense of purpose. By defining specific objectives and committing to their achievement, individuals can maintain focus and motivation throughout the program.

The power of consistency and habit formation is another critical element of the 75 Day Challenge Program. Consistency is the driving force behind lasting change, and by developing positive habits, individuals can significantly improve various aspects of their lives. The program is designed to help participants build these habits through daily activities and practices, reinforcing the importance of consistency in achieving personal transformation.

As participants embark on the 75 Day Challenge Program, they will be guided through a series of daily tasks and activities designed to promote mental strength and discipline. These tasks may initially appear challenging or even daunting, but with persistence and dedication, they will become more manageable and, eventually, a natural part of one's daily routine. The key to success in this program lies in embracing the process and understanding that personal growth often requires stepping out of one's comfort zone.

One of the core tenets of the 75 Day Challenge Program is the idea that personal transformation is a gradual, ongoing process. While the program spans 75 days, the habits and skills developed during this time can have a lasting impact far beyond the program's completion. The program is not intended to be a one-time, temporary fix but rather a catalyst for lasting change and continuous self-improvement.

Throughout the 75 Day Challenge Program, participants will be encouraged to maintain an open, reflective mindset. This self-awareness is crucial in identifying areas for growth and recognizing personal achievements along the journey. By continually evaluating one's progress and adjusting goals and strategies as needed, individuals can ensure they are on the right path toward personal transformation.

Another important aspect of the program is the support and encouragement from fellow participants and accountability partners. The journey toward personal growth can be challenging, and having a support network can significantly impact one's motivation and ability to persevere. By sharing experiences, challenges, and successes, individuals can learn from one another and gain valuable insights and perspectives.

Ultimately, the 75 Day Challenge Program is about empowering individuals to take control of their lives, develop mental toughness and discipline, and foster lasting personal growth. By fully committing to the program and its principles, participants can expect to see significant improvements in their physical, mental, and emotional well-being. This journey may not always be easy, but with dedication, persistence, and a willingness to embrace change, the rewards can be truly life-altering.

As the program unfolds, participants will likely encounter obstacles and setbacks. It is essential to approach these challenges with resilience and perseverance, recognizing that growth often occurs through adversity. By cultivating a mindset of determination and adaptability, individuals can overcome these obstacles and continue moving forward on their path to personal transformation.

It is also crucial to recognize that personal growth is a highly individualized process, and each person's journey will be unique. While the 75 Day Challenge

Program provides a structured framework for developing mental toughness and discipline, it is important for participants to tailor the program to their specific needs, goals, and circumstances. By being flexible and open to change, individuals can optimize their experience and maximize the potential for lasting growth.

The 75 Day Challenge Program is an invitation to embark on a transformative journey toward mental strength, discipline, and personal growth. By committing to the program and embracing its principles, participants can unlock their full potential and experience the profound benefits of lasting change. As individuals progress through the program, they will not only develop the habits and skills necessary for success but also gain a deeper understanding of themselves and their capabilities.

In conclusion, the 75 Day Challenge Program is an opportunity to take control of one's life and foster meaningful personal growth. Through the development of mental toughness and discipline, individuals can face challenges with resilience, adapt to change, and ultimately achieve their goals. The journey may not always be easy, but the rewards are well worth the effort. With commitment, consistency, and a willingness to step out of one's comfort zone, personal transformation is not only possible but also inevitable.

The 75 Day Challenge Program is just the beginning of a lifelong journey toward self-improvement and the realization of one's full potential.

Contents

Introduction 1

Chapter 1: Daily Physical Activity 9

Chapter 2: Mindful Nutrition 17

Chapter 3: Personal Growth Activities 23

Chapter 4: Reflection and Self-Awareness 28

Chapter 5: Acts of Kindness 34

Chapter 6: Goal Setting and Commitment 41

Chapter 7: Tracking Progress and Staying Accountable 48

Chapter 8: Building Resilience and Overcoming Challenges 56

Chapter 9: Stress Management and Self-Care 63

Chapter 10: Developing a Growth Mindset 70

Chapter 11: Building and Maintaining Supportive Relationships ... 77

Thank you so much for purchasing and reading my book! I hope you found it valuable and inspiring on your personal growth journey. Your feedback is incredibly important to me and to other readers who may be considering this book.

I kindly ask that you take a moment to leave a review on Amazon to share your thoughts and experiences with the book. Your review will not only help me understand what resonated with you and areas where I can improve but also guide potential readers in their decision-making process.

Your honest feedback is greatly appreciated, and I am truly grateful for your support. Thank you for helping make this book a success and for contributing to the growth of our community of readers.

Wishing you all the best in your personal growth journey.

Chapter 1: Daily Physical Activity

a. The benefits of regular exercise for mental and physical health

Regular exercise offers a multitude of mental and physical health benefits, making it a cornerstone of a healthy lifestyle. Engaging in daily physical activity can lead to improvements in cardiovascular health, muscle strength, endurance, flexibility, and balance, all of which contribute to overall well-being and a reduced risk of developing chronic conditions such as heart disease, diabetes, and certain types of cancer.

In addition to its physical benefits, regular exercise also plays a significant role in promoting mental health. Physical activity has been shown to alleviate stress and anxiety, enhance cognitive function, and boost mood by stimulating the release of endorphins, the body's natural "feel-good" chemicals. Furthermore, consistent exercise can improve sleep quality, increase self-esteem, and foster a greater sense of control over one's life.

b. Different types of exercise and their unique advantages

There is a wide variety of exercise types, each offering unique advantages and benefits. Understanding the different categories of exercise can help individuals tailor their fitness routine to their specific needs and goals.

1. Aerobic exercise: Also known as cardiovascular exercise, aerobic activities involve sustained movement that increases heart rate and breathing. Examples include walking, running, cycling, swimming, and dancing. Aerobic exercise strengthens the heart and lungs, improves circulation, and enhances overall endurance.

2. Strength training: This type of exercise focuses on building muscle strength and endurance through resistance exercises, such as weightlifting, bodyweight exercises, and resistance band workouts. Strength training can improve overall muscle tone, increase metabolism, and promote better bone health.

3. Flexibility training: Stretching and flexibility exercises help to improve the range of motion in

joints and muscles, promoting better posture, reducing the risk of injury, and alleviating muscle tension. Examples of flexibility training include yoga, Pilates, and various stretching routines.

4. Balance training: Balance exercises help improve stability and coordination, which can be particularly beneficial for older adults or individuals recovering from injuries. Examples of balance training activities include tai chi, single-leg exercises, and balance board workouts.

c. Tips for incorporating exercise into your daily routine

Incorporating exercise into your daily routine can be challenging, particularly for those with busy schedules or limited experience with physical activity. However, with a little planning and creativity, it is possible to make exercise a regular part of your life. Here are some tips to help you get started:

1. Set realistic goals: Start by setting achievable goals that align with your current fitness level and lifestyle. Gradually increase the intensity

and duration of your workouts as you become more accustomed to regular exercise.

2. Choose activities you enjoy: Engaging in activities you genuinely enjoy increases the likelihood that you will stick with your exercise routine. Experiment with different types of exercise to find the ones that resonate with you.

3. Schedule your workouts: Treat exercise like an important appointment by scheduling it into your daily routine. Try to find a consistent time each day that works best for you, whether it's in the morning, during lunch, or in the evening.

4. Break it up: If finding a large block of time for exercise is challenging, consider breaking your workouts into smaller, more manageable sessions throughout the day. Even short bursts of physical activity can add up and contribute to your overall fitness.

5. Make it social: Engaging in physical activities with friends or family can make exercise more enjoyable and help keep you accountable to

your goals. Consider joining a group fitness class, sports league, or simply going for a walk with a friend.

d. Overcoming common obstacles to regular physical activity

Despite the numerous benefits of regular exercise, many individuals face obstacles that can make it difficult to maintain a consistent fitness routine. Here are some common challenges and strategies to overcome them:

1. Time constraints: One of the most common obstacles to regular exercise is a lack of time. To combat this issue, consider incorporating short, high-intensity workouts into your routine, which can provide similar benefits to longer, moderate-intensity sessions. Additionally, try to identify opportunities for physical activity throughout the day, such as taking the stairs instead of the elevator or walking or biking to work.

2. Lack of motivation: Maintaining motivation for regular exercise can be challenging. To stay

motivated, set specific, measurable goals and track your progress. Additionally, finding an exercise buddy or joining a group can provide social support and accountability.

3. Physical limitations or injuries: If you are experiencing physical limitations or recovering from an injury, consult with a healthcare professional or fitness expert to develop a safe and appropriate exercise plan. Focus on low-impact activities, such as swimming or cycling, and gradually progress as your strength and mobility improve.

4. Boredom: Doing the same exercises repeatedly can lead to boredom and diminish your motivation to exercise. To combat this issue, try incorporating variety into your fitness routine by exploring different types of exercise, changing your workout environment, or setting new fitness goals.

e. Measuring and tracking your fitness progress

Keeping track of your fitness progress is an essential aspect of maintaining a consistent exercise routine and achieving your goals. Monitoring your progress can help you identify areas for improvement, celebrate your successes, and stay accountable to your goals. Here are some methods for tracking your fitness progress:

1. Keep a workout journal: Record the details of your workouts, including the type of activity, duration, intensity, and any personal reflections or feelings you had during the session. This can help you identify patterns, track improvements, and celebrate milestones.

2. Use a fitness tracker or app: Many fitness trackers and apps can automatically track various aspects of your physical activity, such as steps taken, distance covered, calories burned, and heart rate. These tools can provide valuable insights into your progress and help you stay accountable to your goals.

3. Track specific fitness metrics: Depending on your goals, you may want to track specific metrics related to your exercise performance. For example, if your goal is to improve cardiovascular endurance, you might track your time or distance for a particular aerobic activity. If your goal is to increase strength, you might

track the amount of weight lifted or the number of repetitions completed for specific exercises.

4. Take progress photos: Visual documentation can be a powerful motivator and a helpful tool for tracking your physical progress. Take progress photos at regular intervals, such as every 30 days, to document changes in your physique over time.

5. Perform periodic fitness assessments: Assess your fitness level at regular intervals, such as every six weeks, to measure your progress and make any necessary adjustments to your exercise routine. These assessments might include measuring your resting heart rate, completing a timed mile run or walk, or performing a specific number of push-ups or sit-ups within a set time frame.

In conclusion, daily physical activity is a crucial component of the 75 Day Challenge Program, offering numerous mental and physical health benefits. By understanding the different types of exercise and their unique advantages, incorporating exercise into your daily routine, overcoming common obstacles, and measuring and tracking your progress, you can develop a consistent fitness routine that contributes to your overall success in the program. Embracing daily physical activity will not only improve your health but also enhance your mental resilience and overall quality of life.

Chapter 2: Mindful Nutrition

a. Understanding the importance of nutrition for overall health.

Nutrition plays a vital role in maintaining overall health and well-being. A balanced, nutrient-dense diet provides the body with the essential vitamins, minerals, and macronutrients needed for optimal functioning. Good nutrition supports physical fitness, cognitive function, emotional well-being, and immune health. In the context of the 75 Day Challenge Program, mindful nutrition is essential for fueling your daily physical activities, promoting recovery, and contributing to the development of mental strength and discipline.

b. Key principles of mindful nutrition

Balance: A balanced diet consists of a variety of foods from all food groups, including fruits, vegetables, whole grains, lean proteins, and healthy fats. Consuming a diverse range of foods ensures that you are obtaining all the necessary nutrients to support your health and fitness goals.

Moderation: Mindful nutrition emphasizes the importance of moderation in eating habits. This means avoiding excessive consumption of any one food group or nutrient, as well as limiting the intake of unhealthy, processed foods and added sugars.

Portion control: Learning to recognize appropriate portion sizes for various foods can help prevent overeating and support weight management goals. Use visual cues, such as the size of your palm or a deck of cards, to gauge portion sizes for different food groups.

Mindful eating: Practicing mindful eating involves paying attention to your body's hunger and fullness cues, eating slowly and without distractions, and savoring the flavors and textures of your food. This approach can help improve digestion, reduce overeating, and promote a healthier relationship with food.

c. Strategies for implementing mindful nutrition in daily life.

Plan your meals: Meal planning can help ensure that you are consuming a balanced and nutrient-dense diet while reducing the likelihood of making impulsive, unhealthy food choices. Set aside time each week to plan your meals and grocery list and consider preparing meals in advance to save time and support your nutrition goals.

Read food labels: Familiarize yourself with food labels to better understand the nutritional content of the foods you consume. Look for products with minimal added sugars, unhealthy fats, and artificial ingredients, and choose options that are high in fiber, vitamins, and minerals.

Prioritize whole, minimally processed foods: Focus on consuming whole, minimally processed foods, such as fruits, vegetables, whole grains, lean proteins, and healthy fats. These foods are nutrient-dense and provide the essential vitamins, minerals, and macronutrients needed to support overall health and fitness.

Stay hydrated: Proper hydration is crucial for maintaining overall health, supporting physical performance, and aiding digestion. Aim to drink at least eight 8-ounce glasses of water per day and consider consuming more if you are engaging in intense physical activity or are in a hot environment.

d. Overcoming common challenges in maintaining a healthy diet.

Time constraints: Preparing nutritious meals can be time-consuming, especially for those with busy schedules. To overcome this challenge, consider setting aside time each week to meal prep, invest in kitchen gadgets that can save time, or explore healthy meal delivery services.

Limited access to healthy food options: Living in an area with limited access to fresh, healthy food options can make maintaining a balanced diet challenging. In these situations, consider shopping at local farmers' markets, joining a community-supported agriculture (CSA) program, or ordering groceries online.

Social pressure: Social situations, such as dining out with friends or attending parties, can make sticking to a healthy diet difficult. To navigate these situations, consider reviewing restaurant menus ahead of time to identify healthier options, practicing portion control, and communicating your dietary preferences to your friends and family.

Emotional eating: Emotional eating, or using food as a coping mechanism for stress or negative emotions, can hinder your nutrition goals. To combat this behavior, develop alternative strategies for managing stress, such as practicing mindfulness techniques, engaging in physical activity, or seeking support from friends or a therapist.

e. Tracking your nutrition progress.

Monitoring your dietary habits and progress can help you stay accountable to your nutrition goals and identify areas for improvement. Here are some methods for tracking your nutrition progress:

Keep a food journal: Record the details of your daily food intake, including the type and amount of food consumed, as well as any emotions or thoughts related to your eating habits. This can help you identify patterns and areas for improvement in your diet.

Use a nutrition tracking app: There are numerous nutrition tracking apps available that can help you monitor your daily food intake, track your macronutrient and micronutrient consumption, and set personalized nutrition goals. These apps can be a convenient way to stay accountable and gain insights into your eating habits.

Periodic self-assessment: Reflect on your eating habits and progress regularly, perhaps every few weeks or months, to evaluate whether you are meeting your nutrition goals and maintaining a balanced, nutrient-dense diet. This can help you make any necessary adjustments to your eating habits and stay on track with your overall health and fitness goals.

In conclusion, mindful nutrition is a crucial component of the 75 Day Challenge Program, supporting your physical and mental health as you work towards personal transformation. By understanding the importance of nutrition, implementing key principles, and overcoming common challenges, you can create and maintain a healthy, balanced diet. Additionally, tracking your nutrition progress can help you stay accountable and make informed choices to support your health and well-being throughout the challenge and beyond.

Chapter 3: Personal Growth Activities

a. The significance of personal growth activities in the 75 Day Challenge Program

Personal growth activities are essential elements of the 75 Day Challenge Program, as they help you develop mental strength, resilience, and discipline. By incorporating these activities into your daily routine, you can foster self-awareness, improve your mindset, and cultivate a more fulfilling, purpose-driven life. Personal growth activities encompass a wide range of practices, including reading, journaling, meditation, and goal setting, among others.

b. Reading for personal growth

Benefits of reading: Reading can expand your knowledge, stimulate your imagination, and boost your cognitive abilities. Furthermore, reading self-help or personal development books can provide valuable insights and strategies for improving various aspects of your life, such as relationships, communication, and personal productivity.

Choosing the right books: Select books that align with your personal growth goals, interests, or areas where you would like to improve. Consider recommendations from friends, online reviews, or bestseller lists to find books that resonate with you.

Creating a reading routine: Establish a consistent reading routine by setting aside a specific time each day to read, such as before bed or during your morning commute. Aim to read for at least 20 to 30 minutes per day, and gradually increase the duration if desired.

Applying what you've learned: To maximize the benefits of reading for personal growth, actively apply the insights and techniques you've learned to your daily life. Reflect on how the concepts from the books you've read relate to your personal experiences and consider ways to integrate these ideas into your routine.

c. Journaling for self-reflection and growth

Benefits of journaling: Journaling is a powerful tool for self-reflection, self-discovery, and personal growth. It can help you process your thoughts and emotions, gain clarity on your goals and values, and track your progress throughout the 75 Day Challenge Program.

Types of journaling: There are various forms of journaling, including gratitude journaling, stream-of-consciousness writing, and structured journaling prompts. Experiment with different approaches to find the style that best suits your needs and preferences.

Establishing a journaling routine: Create a consistent journaling routine by setting aside time each day to write. Choose a specific time, such as first thing in the morning or right before bed, to make journaling a habitual part of your daily schedule.

Reviewing and reflecting on your journal entries: Periodically review your journal entries to gain insights into your personal growth journey and identify patterns, achievements, or areas for improvement. Reflect on your experiences and consider how you can apply the lessons learned to continue growing and evolving.

d. Meditation and mindfulness practices

Benefits of meditation: Meditation is a powerful tool for promoting mental clarity, focus, and emotional well-being. Regular meditation can help reduce stress, enhance self-awareness, and improve overall mental and emotional resilience.

Different types of meditation: There are numerous meditation techniques, such as mindfulness meditation, loving-kindness meditation, and body scan meditation, each with their unique benefits and approaches. Experiment with various methods to find the one that best aligns with your personal goals and preferences.

Developing a meditation routine: Establish a regular meditation practice by dedicating a specific time each day to meditate, even if it's just for a few minutes. Find a quiet, comfortable space where you can sit or lie down and focus on your breath or chosen meditation technique.

Incorporating mindfulness into daily life: In addition to formal meditation practice, aim to cultivate mindfulness throughout your daily activities. This can involve paying attention to your thoughts, emotions, and bodily sensations during everyday tasks, such as eating, walking, or conversing with others. Practicing mindfulness can help you become more present and aware, enhancing your overall well-being and personal growth.

e. Goal setting and tracking for personal growth.

The importance of goal setting: Setting clear, specific goals is crucial for personal growth, as it provides direction, motivation, and a sense of purpose. By establishing goals related to the various aspects of your life, such as health, relationships, and career, you can create a roadmap for personal transformation.

SMART goal setting: Utilize the SMART framework (Specific, Measurable, Achievable, Relevant, and Time-bound) to create well-defined, actionable goals. This approach can help you establish realistic objectives and develop a clear plan for achieving them.

Breaking down larger goals: Break larger, long-term goals into smaller, more manageable milestones. This can make the process of working towards your goals feel less overwhelming and help you maintain motivation as you progress.

Tracking your progress: Regularly monitor and evaluate your progress towards your goals. This can involve using a goal-tracking app, maintaining a written log, or periodically reviewing your objectives with a friend or mentor. Tracking your progress can help you stay accountable, identify areas for improvement, and celebrate your achievements.

In conclusion, personal growth activities play a vital role in the 75 Day Challenge Program by fostering self-awareness, mental strength, and resilience. By incorporating practices such as reading, journaling, meditation, and goal setting into your daily routine, you can nurture your personal development and set the stage for lasting transformation.

Chapter 4: Reflection and Self-Awareness

a. The importance of reflection and self-awareness in the 75 Day Challenge Program

Reflection and self-awareness are crucial components of the 75 Day Challenge Program, as they enable you to better understand your thoughts, emotions, and behaviors. Through regular self-reflection, you can gain insights into your strengths and weaknesses, identify areas for improvement, and develop a deeper sense of self-awareness. This process can ultimately help you make more informed choices, cultivate healthier habits, and foster personal growth.

b. Reflective journaling

Benefits of reflective journaling: Reflective journaling is an effective tool for self-discovery and personal growth. By regularly documenting your thoughts, feelings, and experiences, you can gain valuable insights into your mental and emotional patterns, track your progress throughout the challenge, and identify areas for improvement.

Tips for effective reflective journaling: To make the most of reflective journaling, consider setting aside time each day to write about your experiences, thoughts, and emotions. Use open-ended questions or prompts to guide your writing and encourage deeper reflection.

Reviewing your journal entries: Periodically review your journal entries to identify patterns and trends in your thoughts, emotions, and behaviors. Reflect on any recurring themes, challenges, or achievements, and consider how you can use these insights to inform your personal growth journey.

Using your journal as a tool for self-awareness: As you engage in reflective journaling, strive to develop a deeper understanding of your values, beliefs, and motivations. Use your journal entries as a window into your inner world and cultivate greater self-awareness by examining your thoughts and emotions more closely.

c. Mindfulness and self-awareness

The role of mindfulness in self-awareness: Mindfulness is the practice of paying attention to the present moment without judgment. By cultivating mindfulness, you can develop a greater awareness of your thoughts, emotions, and bodily sensations, which can ultimately lead to a deeper understanding of yourself and your personal growth journey.

Practicing mindfulness throughout the day: Incorporate mindfulness into your daily activities by intentionally focusing on the present moment. Pay attention to your thoughts, emotions, and physical sensations as you go about your daily tasks, such as eating, walking, or engaging in conversation.

Mindful meditation for self-awareness: Engage in regular mindful meditation to deepen your self-awareness and enhance your mental clarity. Choose a specific time each day to practice meditation, focusing on your breath or another point of focus. This consistent practice can help you become more attuned to your inner experiences and foster greater self-awareness.

Using mindfulness to identify and manage emotions: By practicing mindfulness, you can develop the ability to recognize and label your emotions as they arise. This awareness can help you manage difficult emotions more effectively and prevent them from negatively impacting your personal growth journey.

d. Self-reflection exercises and techniques

The power of introspection: Introspection is the process of examining your own thoughts, feelings, and motivations. Regular introspection can help you develop a deeper understanding of yourself and your personal growth journey. Set aside time each day to engage in introspection, reflecting on your experiences, emotions, and thought patterns.

Reflection prompts and questions: Use reflection prompts and questions to guide your introspective practice. These prompts can help you explore various aspects of your life, such as your goals, relationships, and personal values. Some examples of reflection prompts include: "What did I learn about myself today?", "What challenges did I face, and how did I handle them?", and "What am I grateful for in my life?"

The role of feedback in self-awareness: Feedback from others can be a valuable tool for self-awareness and personal growth. Actively seek feedback from friends, family, colleagues, or mentors to gain insights into how others perceive you and to identify areas for improvement. Be open to constructive criticism and consider how you can use this feedback to enhance your personal growth journey.

The power of self-assessment tools: Utilize self-assessment tools, such as personality tests, strengths assessments, and values exercises, to gain a deeper understanding of your unique qualities and characteristics. These tools can help you identify your strengths and weaknesses, clarify your values, and uncover your hidden talents and passions.

e. Cultivating self-awareness for lasting personal growth

The importance of self-awareness in personal growth: Developing self-awareness is essential for lasting personal growth, as it allows you to better understand your thoughts, emotions, and behaviors. By cultivating self-awareness, you can make more informed decisions, establish healthier habits, and foster greater resilience in the face of challenges.

Developing self-awareness as an ongoing practice: Recognize that self-awareness is not a one-time achievement, but rather an ongoing process that requires regular reflection and introspection. Continue to engage in self-awareness practices, such as journaling, mindfulness, and introspection, even after the 75 Day Challenge Program has ended.

Embracing change and personal growth: As you cultivate self-awareness, embrace the changes that come with personal growth. Recognize that personal development is a lifelong journey and be open to the transformations that occur as you gain new insights and perspectives about yourself and your life.

The impact of self-awareness on relationships: Developing self-awareness can positively impact your relationships with others. By understanding your own thoughts, emotions, and behaviors, you can communicate more effectively, empathize with others, and navigate interpersonal conflicts with greater skill and understanding.

In conclusion, reflection and self-awareness are critical components of the 75 Day Challenge Program, as they enable you to gain valuable insights into your thoughts, emotions, and behaviors. By engaging in regular self-reflection, mindfulness practices, and introspection, you can cultivate greater self-awareness and set the stage for lasting personal transformation.

Chapter 5: Acts of Kindness

a. The importance of acts of kindness in the 75 Day Challenge Program

Fostering empathy and compassion: Engaging in acts of kindness can help you develop empathy and compassion for others, which are essential qualities for personal growth and overall well-being. By actively seeking out opportunities to be kind and supportive, you can cultivate a deeper sense of connection with others and foster positive emotions within yourself.

The ripple effect of kindness: Acts of kindness can have a powerful ripple effect, as they inspire others to engage in their own acts of kindness. By incorporating acts of kindness into your 75 Day Challenge Program, you can contribute to a more compassionate and connected world.

b. Acts of kindness towards others

Simple acts of kindness: Acts of kindness can be as simple as holding the door for someone, offering a compliment, or lending a listening ear. Look for opportunities to engage in small acts of kindness throughout your day and notice how these acts impact your own mood and well-being.

Volunteer work: Engage in volunteer work as a way to express kindness and give back to your community.

Consider volunteering at a local charity, nonprofit organization, or community center, and explore opportunities to support causes that resonate with your values and interests.

c. Acts of kindness towards yourself

Self-compassion: Practice self-compassion by treating yourself with the same kindness and understanding that you would offer to a friend or loved one. Recognize that everyone makes mistakes and encounters challenges and allow yourself the space to learn and grow from these experiences.

Self-care: Engage in regular self-care activities as a form of kindness towards yourself. Prioritize activities that support your physical, emotional, and mental well-being, such as exercise, proper nutrition, adequate sleep, and relaxation techniques.

d. Tips for incorporating acts of kindness into your daily routine.

Set a daily kindness goal: Set a daily goal to engage in a specific number of acts of kindness, such as three or five acts per day. This can help you stay focused on seeking out opportunities to be kind and supportive to others.

Keep a kindness journal: Maintain a journal in which you record your daily acts of kindness. This can help you reflect on your actions, identify patterns, and gain insights into the impact your kindness has on others and yourself.

e. Overcoming obstacles to acts of kindness.

Time constraints: Many people feel that they are too busy to engage in acts of kindness. To overcome this obstacle, consider incorporating acts of kindness into your existing daily routine. For example, you can offer a compliment to a coworker during a break or hold the door for someone while running errands.

Fear of rejection: Some individuals may hesitate to engage in acts of kindness out of fear that their actions will be rejected or misunderstood. To address this concern, focus on small, genuine acts of kindness that are unlikely to be misconstrued, and remind yourself that your intention is to spread positivity and support.

f. The impact of acts of kindness on personal growth and well-being

Psychological benefits: Engaging in acts of kindness can have significant psychological benefits, such as increased happiness, reduced stress, and improved self-esteem. By incorporating acts of kindness into your 75 Day Challenge Program, you can support your own mental health and well-being while fostering a sense of connection with others.

Creating lasting habits: As you engage in acts of kindness throughout the 75 Day Challenge Program, you may find that these actions become ingrained as lasting habits. By consistently practicing kindness and compassion, you can cultivate a more empathetic and compassionate mindset that will serve you well beyond the duration of the program.

g. The power of gratitude in acts of kindness

Recognizing and appreciating acts of kindness: Developing an attitude of gratitude can help you become more aware of the acts of kindness that others show towards you. By acknowledging and appreciating these gestures, you can deepen your connections with others and cultivate a more positive outlook on life.

Expressing gratitude: Take the time to express gratitude to those who have shown kindness towards you, either through verbal appreciation or written notes. By expressing gratitude, you can further strengthen your relationships and inspire others to continue engaging in acts of kindness.

h. Acts of kindness as a means of personal transformation

The impact on your worldview: Engaging in acts of kindness can fundamentally shift your perspective on the world, fostering a more compassionate and empathetic outlook. As you prioritize kindness and compassion, you may find that your relationships improve, and you become more attuned to the needs and emotions of others.

The role of kindness in self-discovery: As you engage in acts of kindness throughout the 75 Day Challenge Program, you may discover new aspects of yourself, such as previously untapped strengths, passions, or areas for growth. Embrace these revelations as opportunities for personal transformation and self-improvement.

i. Measuring and tracking your acts of kindness.

Setting kindness goals: Establish specific, measurable goals for your acts of kindness, such as engaging in a certain number of acts per day or week. These goals can help you maintain focus and motivation throughout the 75 Day Challenge Program.

Monitoring progress: Track your acts of kindness in a journal or digital app, noting the details of each act and any observations about its impact on others or yourself. Regularly reviewing your progress can help you identify patterns, areas for improvement, and opportunities for growth in your kindness practice.

j. Continuing acts of kindness beyond the 75 Day Challenge Program

Maintaining momentum: As the program concludes, reflect on the impact your acts of kindness have had on your personal growth and well-being. Use these insights to maintain the momentum you have built and continue engaging in acts of kindness as a regular part of your life.

Expanding your kindness practice: Consider exploring new ways to engage in acts of kindness, such as joining a community service group, participating in a charity event, or advocating for social causes that align with your values. By continually expanding your kindness practice, you can continue to grow and evolve as an individual.

Chapter 6: Goal Setting and Commitment

a. The importance of goal setting in personal growth

Direction and focus: Setting goals provides direction and focus for your personal growth journey. By establishing specific objectives, you can channel your energy and resources towards meaningful progress and self-improvement.

Motivation and perseverance: Goals serve as a source of motivation, encouraging you to push through challenges and setbacks. By setting achievable goals and consistently working towards them, you can build resilience and maintain your commitment to personal growth.

b. SMART goals and the 75 Day Challenge Program

Defining SMART goals: SMART goals are Specific, Measurable, Achievable, Relevant, and Time-bound. By setting goals that meet these criteria, you can create a clear roadmap for your personal growth journey throughout the 75 Day Challenge Program.

Aligning SMART goals with the program: As you set your goals for the 75 Day Challenge Program, ensure that they align with the program's core components and principles. This can help you create a comprehensive and cohesive plan for personal transformation.

c. Creating a balanced and holistic approach to goal setting.

Addressing multiple areas of life: When setting goals for the 75 Day Challenge Program, consider addressing multiple areas of your life, such as physical health, mental well-being, relationships, and personal growth. This balanced approach can help you create a well-rounded and holistic plan for personal transformation.

Prioritizing and managing goals: It's essential to prioritize your goals and manage your time and resources effectively. Focus on the most important goals first and break them down into smaller, manageable steps to ensure steady progress throughout the program.

d. The power of commitment and accountability

Making a personal commitment: To succeed in the 75 Day Challenge Program, it's crucial to make a personal commitment to your goals and the growth process. This commitment can serve as a powerful motivator, helping you stay on track and overcome obstacles along the way.

Establishing accountability: To enhance your commitment, consider establishing accountability mechanisms, such as sharing your goals with a trusted friend or family member, joining a support group, or using a goal-tracking app. These strategies can help you stay accountable to your goals and maintain motivation throughout the program.

e. Adapting and adjusting goals as needed

Embracing flexibility: Although it's important to stay committed to your goals, it's also crucial to remain flexible and open to change. Recognize that your goals may need to be adjusted as you progress through the 75 Day Challenge Program and encounter new challenges or insights.

Regularly reviewing and revising goals: Schedule periodic check-ins to review and assess your goals throughout the program. Use these check-ins to celebrate your successes, identify areas for improvement, and make any necessary adjustments to your goals.

f. Overcoming setbacks and obstacles in goal achievement.

Anticipating challenges: Recognize that setbacks and obstacles are a natural part of the personal growth process. Anticipate potential challenges and develop strategies for overcoming them, such as seeking support, reevaluating your goals, or adjusting your approach.

Learning from setbacks: Instead of viewing setbacks as failures, consider them as opportunities for growth and learning. Reflect on the lessons you can draw from each setback and use these insights to inform your future goal-setting and personal growth efforts.

g. Celebrating successes and milestones

Acknowledging progress: As you work towards your goals throughout the 75 Day Challenge Program, take time to acknowledge your progress and celebrate your successes. Celebrating milestones, big or small, can help you stay motivated and inspired throughout the program.

Finding inspiration and support: Consider seeking inspiration and support from others as you celebrate your successes. Share your accomplishments with trusted friends or family members, join a support group, or connect with other participants in the 75 Day Challenge Program.

h. Reflection and adjustment post-75 Day Challenge Program

Reflecting on your personal growth journey: After completing the 75 Day Challenge Program, take time to reflect on your personal growth journey. Consider the progress you made towards your goals and any insights or learnings you gained throughout the program.

Planning for continued growth and maintenance: As you reflect on your personal growth journey, consider how you can continue to build on the progress you made during the program. Develop a plan for ongoing growth and maintenance, setting new goals and adjusting your approach as needed.

i. The importance of mindset in goal achievement

Cultivating a growth mindset: Developing a growth mindset can be a powerful tool for achieving your goals. Embrace challenges and setbacks as opportunities for growth and learning and believe in your ability to improve and make progress.

Overcoming limiting beliefs: Recognize and challenge any limiting beliefs or self-doubt that may be holding you back from achieving your goals. Reframe negative thoughts into positive, empowering affirmations that help you stay focused and motivated.

j. Tips for staying motivated and committed to your goals.

Visualizing success: Use visualization techniques to imagine yourself achieving your goals and living the life you desire. This can help you stay motivated and focused on your vision for personal growth and transformation.

Finding inspiration: Look for sources of inspiration and motivation that resonate with you, such as inspiring quotes, uplifting music, or motivational speakers. Use these sources to stay inspired and energized throughout the 75 Day Challenge Program.

In summary, goal setting and commitment are critical components of the 75 Day Challenge Program. By creating balanced and holistic goals, making a personal commitment, adapting to challenges, celebrating successes, and maintaining a growth mindset, you can achieve meaningful personal growth and transformation during the program and beyond.

Chapter 7: Tracking Progress and Staying Accountable

The Benefits of Tracking Progress and Maintaining Accountability

Tracking your progress and maintaining accountability throughout the 75 Day Challenge Program are essential components for success. By consistently monitoring your progress, you can ensure you stay focused on your goals and make timely adjustments as needed. This ongoing evaluation helps you to stay on track and maximize your efforts.

Accountability is equally important, as it keeps you motivated and committed to your personal growth journey. Holding yourself accountable means being responsible for your actions, decisions, and progress. This sense of responsibility helps you stay disciplined and focused, making it more likely for you to achieve your goals.

Some of the key benefits of tracking progress and maintaining accountability include:

Increased motivation: When you see progress, it reinforces your commitment and motivates you to continue working towards your goals.

Enhanced self-awareness: Tracking your progress helps you better understand your strengths and weaknesses, enabling you to make informed decisions about your personal growth journey.

Improved decision-making: By consistently monitoring your progress, you can identify areas where adjustments need to be made, helping you to make better decisions that align with your goals.

Greater resilience: Holding yourself accountable for your actions and decisions builds resilience, making it easier to overcome challenges and setbacks along the way.

Higher likelihood of success: Research shows that individuals who track their progress and maintain accountability are more likely to achieve their goals than those who do not.

Tools and Techniques for Tracking Your Progress in Various Aspects of the Program

There are numerous tools and techniques available to help you track your progress in different aspects of the 75 Day Challenge Program. These methods can be easily customized to your preferences and needs. Here are some suggestions:

Journaling: Keeping a daily journal is a powerful way to document your thoughts, emotions, and achievements throughout the program. You can use this tool to record your progress in various areas, including exercise, nutrition, personal growth activities, acts of kindness, and goal setting.

Mobile apps: Many apps are available that can help you track your progress in various domains, such as fitness, nutrition, and goal setting. Choose one that best suits your needs and preferences and use it consistently to stay on track.

Spreadsheets: Create a custom spreadsheet to track your progress in different aspects of the program. You can design it to record daily activities, achievements, and reflections.

Visual representations: Consider creating visual representations of your progress, such as charts, graphs, or vision boards. These tools can provide a clear, at-a-glance overview of your journey and inspire you to keep pushing forward.

Habit trackers: Utilize habit-tracking tools, whether digital or paper-based, to monitor your consistency in performing daily activities related to the program.

The Role of Social Support and Accountability Partners

Social support and accountability partners can be invaluable resources on your personal growth journey. They provide encouragement, motivation, and guidance while also holding you accountable for your actions and commitments.

To make the most of social support, consider sharing your goals and progress with friends, family members, or coworkers who understand and support your aspirations. Alternatively, you may choose to join online forums, social media groups, or local meetups that focus on personal growth and self-improvement.

Accountability partners can take various forms, including mentors, coaches, or peers who share similar goals. By regularly checking in with your accountability partner, you can discuss your progress, challenges, and achievements, and receive valuable feedback and guidance.

Benefits of having an accountability partner include:

Increased motivation: Knowing that someone else is following your progress can provide an extra boost of motivation to stay committed to your goals.

2. Objective feedback: An accountability partner can offer objective feedback, helping you identify areas for improvement and providing guidance on how to make adjustments.

Shared experiences: Having someone who understands the challenges and joys of personal growth can make the journey more enjoyable and fulfilling.

Emotional support: An accountability partner can provide emotional support during tough times, helping you stay focused and committed.

Increased likelihood of success: Studies have shown that individuals with accountability partners are more likely to achieve their goals than those who go it alone.

Adjusting Your Approach Based on Progress and Feedback

As you progress through the 75 Day Challenge Program, it's essential to remain open to adjusting your approach based on your progress and feedback. Regularly evaluate your goals and strategies to ensure they are still relevant, achievable, and aligned with your overall vision.

Listen to the feedback and insights provided by your accountability partners, mentors, and peers. They can offer valuable perspectives on your journey and suggest potential improvements or adjustments.

Finally, always be willing to learn from your setbacks and challenges. Use these experiences as opportunities for growth and refinement, adapting your approach as needed to better suit your evolving needs and aspirations.

Key steps to effectively adjust your approach include:

Reflect on your progress: Take time to evaluate your achievements, setbacks, and growth areas, identifying patterns and areas where adjustments may be needed.

Seek feedback: Ask for feedback from your accountability partners, mentors, and peers to gain additional insights and perspectives.

Be flexible: Embrace the idea of making changes to your plan, understanding that adjustments are a natural part of personal growth and development.

Set new goals: As you progress, reassess your goals and set new ones that align with your current situation and aspirations.

Stay committed: Remember your "why" and stay committed to your personal growth journey, even when challenges arise.

Staying Motivated and Committed Throughout the 75 Day Challenge Program

Maintaining motivation and commitment throughout the 75 Day Challenge Program is crucial for success. Here are a few strategies to help you stay focused and determined:

Establish a strong "why": Understanding the underlying reasons for your personal growth journey can serve as a powerful motivator. Keep your "why" at the forefront of your mind to remind you of the importance of staying committed to your goals.

Set realistic expectations: Avoid setting overly ambitious goals that may be difficult to achieve. Instead, focus on setting realistic, attainable goals that still challenge and inspire you.

Celebrate small victories: Acknowledge and celebrate your accomplishments, no matter how small they may seem. This practice helps to maintain your motivation and reinforces your commitment to the program.

Surround yourself with positive influences: Spend time with people who inspire, support, and encourage your personal growth journey. Their positivity can help keep you motivated and focused.

Practice self-compassion: Be kind to yourself during the process, understanding that setbacks and challenges are a natural part of growth. Treat yourself with compassion and patience, and use these experiences as opportunities to learn and grow.

By implementing these strategies and staying committed to tracking your progress and maintaining accountability, you will be well on your way to achieving lasting personal growth and transformation through the 75 Day Challenge Program.

Chapter 8: Building Resilience and Overcoming Challenges

The Importance of Resilience in Personal Growth

Resilience is the ability to bounce back from adversity and adapt to challenges, making it an essential component of personal growth. Building resilience equips you with the mental and emotional tools needed to navigate setbacks and obstacles on your journey, ultimately fostering a more robust sense of self and well-being.

The importance of resilience in personal growth lies in its ability to:

Enhance mental and emotional strength: Resilient individuals are better equipped to handle stress, setbacks, and disappointments, maintaining a positive outlook even in the face of adversity.

Foster personal growth: Challenges provide opportunities for growth and self-discovery. Embracing these experiences and learning from them can lead to significant personal development.

Improve problem-solving skills: Resilience enables you to approach challenges with a solution-oriented mindset, enhancing your ability to navigate difficult situations.

Promote self-confidence: Overcoming challenges and bouncing back from setbacks can boost your self-confidence and belief in your abilities.

Encourage perseverance: Resilient individuals are more likely to persevere in the face of adversity, making it more likely for them to achieve their personal growth goals.

Strategies for Building Resilience

There are several strategies you can employ to build resilience and better cope with challenges on your personal growth journey. Here are a few suggestions:

Develop a growth mindset: Embrace the idea that setbacks and failures are opportunities for growth and learning, rather than a reflection of your worth or abilities.

Cultivate self-awareness: Developing a deep understanding of your emotions, strengths, and weaknesses can help you better navigate challenges and adapt to adversity.

Practice self-compassion: Treat yourself with kindness and understanding, recognizing that setbacks and difficulties are a natural part of life and personal growth.

Establish a strong support network: Surround yourself with people who support, encourage, and understand your personal growth journey, providing you with valuable emotional and practical support.

Focus on what you can control: In the face of adversity, focus on the aspects of the situation that you can control, rather than dwelling on factors beyond your influence.

Identifying and Overcoming Common Personal Growth Challenges

Throughout your personal growth journey, you may encounter various challenges and obstacles. Being able to identify and address these common challenges can help you stay on track and maintain your resilience.

Fear of failure: Many people struggle with the fear of failure, which can hinder their progress and prevent them from taking risks. To overcome this fear, reframe your perspective on failure as a learning opportunity rather than a negative outcome. Embrace the lessons that failure can teach you and use them to grow and improve.

Procrastination: Procrastination can significantly impede your personal growth journey by delaying your progress and causing you to lose momentum. To combat procrastination, break tasks into smaller, more manageable steps, and establish a consistent routine to help you stay focused and on track.

Self-doubt: Self-doubt can undermine your confidence and prevent you from pursuing your goals. To overcome self-doubt, focus on your strengths and accomplishments, and remind yourself of your past successes. Surround yourself with positive influences that can boost your confidence and encourage your personal growth journey.

Lack of motivation: Maintaining motivation throughout your personal growth journey can be challenging, especially during difficult periods. To sustain your motivation, connect with your "why" – the underlying reasons behind your personal growth goals – and revisit it regularly to remind yourself of its importance. Celebrate your achievements, both big and small, and seek inspiration from others who have overcome similar challenges.

Time management: Finding the time to dedicate to your personal growth can be difficult, especially with other life commitments. To effectively manage your time, prioritize your personal growth goals and allocate specific time slots in your daily schedule for related activities. Utilize time management tools and techniques, such as to-do lists and calendar apps, to help you stay organized and focused on your priorities.

Developing a Resilient Mindset

Developing a resilient mindset is crucial to overcoming challenges and maintaining progress in your personal growth journey. Here are some tips for cultivating a resilient mindset:

Embrace change: Accept that change is a natural part of life and personal growth. Rather than resisting change, learn to adapt and grow from new experiences and challenges.

Develop emotional intelligence: Emotional intelligence is the ability to recognize, understand, and manage your own emotions and those of others. By developing emotional intelligence, you can better navigate difficult situations and maintain a positive outlook.

Practice gratitude: Cultivate an attitude of gratitude by regularly acknowledging the positive aspects of your life and experiences. This practice can help to shift your focus away from challenges and setbacks, promoting a more optimistic outlook.

Maintain a sense of humor: A healthy sense of humor can help you keep challenges and setbacks in perspective, allowing you to cope more effectively with adversity.

Stay solution-focused: When faced with challenges, focus on finding solutions rather than dwelling on the problem. This approach encourages a proactive mindset, which can ultimately lead to more effective problem-solving and personal growth.

Applying Resilience to Overcome Challenges in the 75 Day Challenge Program

As you progress through the 75 Day Challenge Program, applying resilience to overcome challenges is essential for success. Here are some ways to apply resilience in your personal growth journey:

Reflect on past experiences: Draw on your past experiences of overcoming challenges to remind yourself of your resilience and ability to adapt.

Seek support: Reach out to your support network, including accountability partners, friends, and family members, for encouragement and guidance during difficult times.

Reevaluate your goals: If you encounter significant obstacles or setbacks, take the time to reevaluate your goals and make adjustments as needed. This can help you stay focused and committed to your personal growth journey, even in the face of adversity.

Practice self-care: Ensure you're taking care of your physical, mental, and emotional well-being throughout the program. Prioritize self-care activities, such as exercise, sleep, and relaxation, to help maintain your resilience and overall health.

Stay persistent: Despite setbacks and challenges, remain persistent in your pursuit of personal growth. Remember that the journey is just as important as the destination, and by building resilience, you're better equipped to overcome challenges and achieve your goals.

By developing resilience and learning to overcome challenges, you will be better prepared to navigate your personal growth journey and successfully complete the 75 Day Challenge Program. Embrace the opportunity for growth that challenges provide, and use the strategies outlined in this chapter to build your resilience and achieve lasting personal transformation.

Chapter 9: Stress Management and Self-Care

The Importance of Stress Management and Self-Care

Stress management and self-care are essential components of a successful personal growth journey. They help to maintain your physical, mental, and emotional well-being, which ultimately supports your ability to pursue your goals and overcome challenges. By prioritizing stress management and self-care, you can:

Improve overall health: Reducing stress and taking care of your body can lead to improved physical health, including better sleep, increased energy levels, and a stronger immune system.

Enhance emotional well-being: Self-care practices can help to reduce feelings of anxiety, depression, and stress, promoting emotional balance and resilience.

Increase productivity: Managing stress and practicing self-care can result in increased focus, better decision-making, and improved time management, all of which contribute to greater productivity.

Foster a positive mindset: Taking care of yourself and managing stress can help to cultivate a more positive outlook, making it easier to stay committed to your personal growth journey.

Strengthen relationships: When you prioritize your own well-being, you are better equipped to engage in healthy and supportive relationships with others.

Identifying Sources of Stress

Recognizing the sources of stress in your life is the first step toward effective stress management. By identifying what causes stress for you, you can develop targeted strategies for addressing and reducing these stressors. Common sources of stress include:

Work-related stress: Demanding workloads, tight deadlines, and challenging work environments can contribute to significant stress.

Financial stress: Money-related concerns, such as debt, living expenses, or financial instability, can be a major source of stress.

Relationship stress: Interpersonal conflicts or challenges within your relationships can lead to increased stress levels.

Health-related stress: Chronic illnesses, injuries, or other health concerns can be both physically and emotionally stressful.

Time management stress: Juggling multiple responsibilities and commitments can lead to feelings of stress and overwhelm.

Take some time to reflect on the specific sources of stress in your life, as this will enable you to develop targeted strategies for managing and reducing their impact on your well-being.

Stress Management Techniques

There are numerous stress management techniques that you can incorporate into your daily routine to help reduce stress and promote overall well-being. Some effective stress management techniques include:

Exercise: Regular physical activity can help to reduce stress, improve mood, and increase energy levels.

Mindfulness and meditation: Practicing mindfulness and meditation can help to promote relaxation, focus, and emotional balance.

Deep breathing exercises: Deep, controlled breathing can help to activate your body's relaxation response and reduce feelings of stress and anxiety.

Time management strategies: Effective time management can help to alleviate stress by ensuring that you have adequate time to complete tasks and maintain a healthy work-life balance.

Social support: Connecting with friends, family, and other supportive individuals can help to alleviate stress by providing emotional support, practical assistance, and opportunities for relaxation and enjoyment.

Experiment with different stress management techniques to find those that work best for you, and incorporate them into your daily routine to help maintain your overall well-being.

Self-Care Practices

Self-care is the practice of taking care of your physical, mental, and emotional well-being. By incorporating self-care practices into your daily routine, you can support your overall health and maintain the resilience and energy needed to pursue your personal growth goals. Some self-care practices to consider include:

Regular exercise: Engaging in physical activity on a regular basis can help to improve your physical health and mental well-being.

Adequate sleep: Ensuring that you get sufficient, high-quality sleep is essential for maintaining your physical and emotional health, as well as your ability to focus and be productive.

Healthy diet: Consuming a balanced, nutritious diet can help to support your overall health, energy levels, and mood.

Social connections: Prioritize spending time with friends, family, and other supportive individuals to foster meaningful connections and maintain emotional well-being.

Relaxation techniques: Incorporate relaxation techniques, such as deep breathing exercises, meditation, or progressive muscle relaxation, into your daily routine to help reduce stress and promote a sense of calm.

Hobbies and interests: Engage in activities that bring you joy, satisfaction, and a sense of accomplishment, whether it be creative pursuits, sports, or other hobbies.

Set boundaries: Establish and maintain healthy boundaries in your personal and professional life to ensure you have adequate time and energy for self-care and personal growth.

Regular check-ins: Take time each day or week to check in with yourself and assess your physical, mental, and emotional well-being. This can help you to identify areas where you may need to focus more attention or make adjustments in your self-care practices.

Incorporating Stress Management and Self-Care into the 75 Day Challenge Program

As you progress through the 75 Day Challenge Program, it is essential to prioritize stress management and self-care to support your overall well-being and personal growth journey. Here are some tips for incorporating these practices into the program:

Schedule time for self-care: Allocate specific time slots in your daily or weekly schedule for self-care activities, such as exercise, relaxation, or social connections.

Set realistic expectations: Establish realistic goals and expectations for your personal growth journey, and recognize that setbacks and challenges are a natural part of the process.

Maintain a balanced lifestyle: Strive to maintain a healthy balance between your personal growth goals, work, and personal life, ensuring that you have adequate time and energy for all aspects of your life.

Seek support: Reach out to your support network, including accountability partners, friends, and family members, for encouragement and guidance during challenging times.

Monitor and adjust: Regularly assess your stress levels and self-care practices, making adjustments as needed to ensure that you are effectively managing stress and maintaining your overall well-being.

By incorporating stress management and self-care practices into your 75 Day Challenge Program, you can enhance your overall well-being, resilience, and ability to achieve your personal growth goals. Prioritize these practices and be mindful of their impact on your journey, as they play a crucial role in supporting your lasting personal transformation.

Chapter 10: Developing a Growth Mindset

Understanding the Growth Mindset

A growth mindset is a belief that your abilities, intelligence, and talents can be developed and improved through hard work, dedication, and perseverance. This mindset is contrasted with a fixed mindset, which assumes that your traits and abilities are fixed and unchangeable. By adopting a growth mindset, you can:

Foster a love of learning: A growth mindset encourages curiosity, exploration, and a willingness to learn from mistakes, fostering a lifelong love of learning.

Increase resilience: Believing in your ability to grow and improve allows you to better cope with challenges and setbacks, enhancing your overall resilience.

Improve motivation: With a growth mindset, you are more likely to set challenging goals and stay committed to achieving them, as you believe in your capacity for growth and improvement.

Enhance performance: Studies have shown that individuals with a growth mindset perform better in various areas of life, including academics, sports, and professional pursuits.

Foster healthier relationships: A growth mindset can lead to more constructive communication, empathy, and understanding in relationships, as you recognize that both you and others have the potential to grow and change.

Identifying Fixed Mindset Triggers

To develop a growth mindset, it's important to first identify the triggers that lead to fixed mindset thinking. These triggers may manifest as negative thoughts, self-doubt, or self-limiting beliefs. Some common fixed mindset triggers include:

Fear of failure: Believing that failure is a reflection of your inherent abilities, rather than an opportunity for growth and learning.

Comparison to others: Measuring your worth and abilities based on the achievements and successes of others.

Perfectionism: Believing that you must always perform at your best and never make mistakes.

Dismissive attitude towards feedback: Interpreting feedback or criticism as an attack on your abilities, rather than an opportunity for growth.

Resistance to change: Believing that you are unable to adapt or grow in response to new challenges or situations.

By identifying these triggers, you can begin to recognize when your fixed mindset is holding you back and actively work to shift your thinking toward a growth mindset.

Strategies for Developing a Growth Mindset

Once you have identified your fixed mindset triggers, you can implement various strategies to cultivate a growth mindset. Some of these strategies include:

Embrace challenges: View challenges as opportunities for growth and learning, rather than as threats to your abilities or self-worth.

Learn from mistakes: Recognize that mistakes are a natural part of the learning process and use them as opportunities to grow and improve.

Practice self-compassion: Be kind and understanding with yourself when you encounter setbacks or difficulties, acknowledging that growth and progress are often accompanied by challenges.

Seek feedback: Actively seek out feedback from others and use it constructively to identify areas for growth and improvement.

Cultivate a positive inner dialogue: Replace self-limiting thoughts and beliefs with positive affirmations and self-talk that encourages growth and learning.

By consistently practicing these strategies, you can gradually shift your mindset from a fixed perspective to one that embraces growth and development.

Applying a Growth Mindset to the 75 Day Challenge Program

As you progress through the 75 Day Challenge Program, adopting a growth mindset can significantly enhance your personal growth journey. Here are some tips for applying a growth mindset to the program:

Set realistic, yet challenging goals: Establish goals that push you to grow and develop, while also being mindful of your current abilities and limitations.

Embrace setbacks and obstacles: Recognize that challenges and setbacks are a natural part of the personal growth journey and use them as opportunities to learn and adapt.

Maintain a positive attitude: Cultivate a positive outlook and focus on the progress you are making, rather than dwelling on perceived failures or shortcomings.

Celebrate small victories: Acknowledge and celebrate your incremental achievements and improvements, recognizing that each step contributes to your overall growth and development.

Reflect on your growth: Regularly assess your progress and growth throughout the program, and use this reflection to inform your future goals and strategies.

By applying a growth mindset to your 75 Day Challenge Program, you can enhance your motivation, resilience, and overall personal growth experience.

Sustaining a Growth Mindset Beyond the 75 Day Challenge Program

Developing and maintaining a growth mindset is a lifelong process that extends beyond the 75 Day Challenge Program. Here are some tips for sustaining a growth mindset throughout your life:

Continuously seek new challenges: Actively pursue new experiences, skills, and opportunities for growth and development, even after you have completed the 75 Day Challenge Program.

Surround yourself with growth-minded individuals: Cultivate relationships with people who share your growth mindset and can provide encouragement, support, and inspiration for continued growth.

Stay open to feedback: Maintain an open and receptive attitude toward feedback and criticism, using it as a valuable resource for personal growth and improvement.

Emphasize learning and personal development: Prioritize ongoing learning and self-improvement in all aspects of your life, recognizing that growth is a continuous process.

Practice self-compassion and patience: Be patient with yourself and practice self-compassion as you continue to grow and develop, acknowledging that the journey of personal growth is a lifelong process.

By incorporating these strategies into your daily life, you can maintain a growth mindset that supports your ongoing personal growth and self-improvement journey. With a growth mindset as the foundation, you can continue to develop your abilities, intelligence, and talents, maximizing your potential and fostering a fulfilling and meaningful life.

Chapter 11: Building and Maintaining Supportive Relationships

The Importance of Supportive Relationships

Supportive relationships play a crucial role in our overall well-being, personal growth, and success. These relationships, which can include friendships, family connections, and romantic partnerships, provide us with emotional support, encouragement, and a sense of belonging. By cultivating and maintaining strong, healthy relationships, you can experience numerous benefits, such as:

Enhanced mental and emotional well-being: Supportive relationships can help reduce feelings of loneliness, anxiety, and depression, and contribute to a greater sense of self-worth and happiness.

Improved physical health: Studies have shown that individuals with strong social connections tend to have better overall health, as well as lower rates of chronic illnesses and longer life expectancies.

Increased resilience: Having a solid support network can help you better cope with life's challenges and setbacks, and bounce back more quickly from difficult situations.

Greater personal growth and development: Supportive relationships can encourage personal growth, as they provide us with the motivation, inspiration, and guidance necessary to pursue our goals and dreams.

Enhanced communication skills: Building and maintaining strong relationships requires effective communication, which in turn can improve your ability to connect with others and express your thoughts and emotions.

As you progress through your personal growth journey, including the 75 Day Challenge Program, it is essential to prioritize building and maintaining supportive relationships to enhance your overall well-being and success.

Identifying and Cultivating Supportive Relationships

To build and maintain supportive relationships, it is essential first to identify the characteristics of such relationships and seek out individuals who exhibit these qualities. Some key traits of supportive relationships include:

Trust and reliability: Supportive relationships are built on a foundation of trust, with both parties being reliable and consistent in their actions and communication.

Open communication: Healthy relationships involve open, honest, and respectful communication, allowing for the expression of thoughts, feelings, and concerns.

Empathy and understanding: Supportive individuals demonstrate empathy and understanding, striving to see situations from your perspective and validating your feelings and experiences.

Encouragement and motivation: Supportive relationships involve mutual encouragement and motivation, with both parties inspiring and uplifting each other in their personal growth journeys.

Respect and acceptance: In a supportive relationship, both individuals respect and accept each other for who they are, without attempting to change or control the other person.

Once you have identified the characteristics of supportive relationships, you can begin to cultivate these connections by:

Engaging in social activities: Participate in social events, clubs, or organizations that align with your interests and values to meet like-minded individuals.

Reaching out to existing connections: Strengthen your existing relationships by reaching out to friends, family members, or colleagues and expressing your desire for deeper, more supportive connections.

Developing your communication skills: Work on improving your communication skills, including active listening, empathy, and assertiveness, to foster deeper connections with others.

Setting boundaries: Establish and maintain healthy boundaries in your relationships to ensure that your needs are met, and you have the time and energy necessary for personal growth and self-care.

Providing support to others: Offer encouragement, understanding, and assistance to those in your life, demonstrating the qualities of a supportive individual and fostering reciprocal relationships.

Nurturing Supportive Relationships

Once you have identified and cultivated supportive relationships, it's essential to put in the effort to nurture and maintain these connections. Here are some strategies to help you strengthen and deepen your supportive relationships:

Prioritize quality time: Make time for regular face-to-face interactions, phone calls, or video chats to maintain a close connection and stay involved in each other's lives.

Show appreciation: Express gratitude for the support, encouragement, and understanding your loved ones provide, acknowledging the positive impact they have on your life.

Be an active listener: When your loved ones share their thoughts, feelings, or experiences, practice active listening by giving them your full attention, asking questions, and validating their emotions.

Offer support: Be there for your loved ones in times of need, providing emotional support, practical assistance, or simply a listening ear.

Celebrate successes: Share in the joy of your loved ones' accomplishments, and celebrate their achievements and personal growth.

Encourage personal growth: Support and encourage your loved ones in their personal growth journeys, offering guidance, motivation, and resources as needed.

Maintain open communication: Keep the lines of communication open, discussing any concerns or issues that arise in the relationship and working together to find solutions.

By consistently nurturing and investing in your supportive relationships, you can create strong, lasting connections that contribute significantly to your personal growth journey and overall well-being.

Balancing Personal Growth with Supportive Relationships

As you continue on your personal growth journey, it is essential to strike a balance between focusing on your own development and maintaining supportive relationships. Some tips for achieving this balance include:

Schedule regular check-ins: Set aside dedicated time to connect with your loved ones, ensuring that your relationships remain a priority even as you work on personal growth.

Share your goals and progress: Keep your loved ones informed about your personal growth journey, discussing your goals, challenges, and successes to maintain a sense of connection and support.

Seek feedback and advice: Involve your loved ones in your personal growth process by seeking their feedback, insights, and advice on your goals, strategies, and progress.

Engage in joint growth activities: Participate in personal growth activities together, such as attending workshops, reading books, or engaging in mindfulness practices, to strengthen your relationships while also fostering individual growth.

Maintain boundaries: Establish and maintain healthy boundaries that allow you to focus on your personal growth while still being present and supportive in your relationships.

The Role of Supportive Relationships in Long-Term Personal Growth

Supportive relationships play a crucial role in fostering long-term personal growth and can significantly impact your overall well-being and success. By building and maintaining strong, healthy connections with others, you can ensure that your personal growth journey is sustainable and fulfilling. Here are some ways that supportive relationships contribute to your long-term personal growth:

Provide motivation and encouragement: Supportive relationships offer a source of motivation and encouragement, helping you maintain momentum and stay focused on your personal growth goals.

Offer new perspectives and insights: Engaging with supportive individuals can expose you to new perspectives and ideas, broadening your understanding of yourself and the world around you.

Promote accountability: Supportive relationships can help you stay accountable to your personal growth goals, providing the encouragement and guidance needed to stay on track and make progress.

Serve as a source of resilience: When you face challenges or setbacks in your personal growth journey, supportive relationships can provide the emotional support and understanding needed to persevere and overcome obstacles.

Foster the development of important skills: Supportive relationships can help you develop essential skills, such as communication, empathy, and problem-solving, which contribute to your overall personal growth and development.

As you continue on your personal growth journey, be sure to prioritize building and maintaining supportive relationships, recognizing the significant impact they have on your overall well-being and success. By investing in these connections, you can create a strong support network that not only enhances your personal growth but also contributes to a more fulfilling and meaningful life.

In conclusion, building and maintaining supportive relationships is a critical component of personal growth and overall well-being. By identifying and cultivating connections with individuals who demonstrate trust, open communication, empathy, encouragement, and respect, you can create a solid foundation for long-term growth and success. As you progress through the 75 Day Challenge Program and beyond, be sure to prioritize nurturing your supportive relationships and striking a balance between personal growth and connection with others. Through these efforts, you will not only enhance your own personal growth journey but also contribute to the growth and well-being of those around you.

Reflecting on Your Personal Growth Journey

As you reach the end of the 75 Day Challenge Program and reflect on your personal growth journey, take the time to consider the progress you have made and the insights you have gained. Remember that personal growth is an ongoing process, and the skills, habits, and mindset you have developed during the program will serve you well in your future endeavors. Some key areas to reflect upon include:

Mental and physical well-being: Assess the impact of the program on your mental and physical health, considering improvements in areas such as stress management, mood, energy levels, and overall fitness.

Personal growth activities: Reflect on the personal growth activities you engaged in during the program, evaluating their effectiveness and identifying any areas where you would like to continue focusing.

Goal setting and commitment: Review the goals you set at the beginning of the program, celebrating your achievements and considering any adjustments needed for future goal-setting.

Supportive relationships: Evaluate the strength and quality of your supportive relationships, recognizing their impact on your personal growth journey and identifying opportunities for further development.

Resilience and overcoming challenges: Consider the obstacles and challenges you faced during the program, reflecting on the strategies you used to overcome them and the lessons you learned along the way.

Recognizing the Lasting Impact of Mental Strength and Discipline

The 75 Day Challenge Program has provided you with the opportunity to develop mental strength and discipline, qualities that will have a lasting impact on your life. These attributes not only contribute to your success in the program but also serve as a foundation for overcoming future challenges and pursuing personal growth in all aspects of your life. Some of the lasting impacts of mental strength and discipline include:

Increased self-confidence: By developing mental strength and discipline, you have demonstrated your ability to set and achieve goals, resulting in greater self-confidence and belief in your capabilities.

Enhanced resilience: Mental strength and discipline help you cultivate resilience, equipping you to face challenges and setbacks with courage and determination.

Improved decision-making: Mental discipline allows you to make more thoughtful, intentional decisions, contributing to better outcomes in both your personal and professional life.

Greater focus and productivity: By practicing discipline and mental strength, you can improve your ability to focus and stay on task, leading to increased productivity and efficiency.

Stronger relationships: Mental strength and discipline can improve your communication and conflict resolution skills, fostering healthier and more supportive relationships.

As you move forward beyond the 75 Day Challenge Program, remember the lasting impact of mental strength and discipline and continue to cultivate these qualities in your daily life.

Maintaining the Habits and Lessons Learned Beyond the 75 Day Challenge Program

Although the 75 Day Challenge Program may have come to an end, the habits and lessons you have learned during this time can continue to serve you in your ongoing personal growth journey. To maintain the progress you have made and continue to build upon your successes, consider the following strategies:

Set new goals: Continue to set clear, achievable goals for yourself, focusing on areas where you would like to see further growth and development.

Stay accountable: Maintain accountability for your personal growth by tracking your progress, setting deadlines, and seeking feedback from supportive individuals.

Prioritize self-care: Continue to prioritize self-care and stress management practices, ensuring that you have the physical and emotional resources necessary to pursue your goals.

Engage in lifelong learning: Seek out new opportunities for personal growth and development, whether through reading, workshops, online courses, or other learning experiences.

Nurture supportive relationships: Continue to invest in your supportive relationships, recognizing their crucial role in your overall well-being and personal growth journey.

By maintaining the habits and lessons learned during the 75 Day Challenge Program, you can ensure that your personal growth journey continues to be fulfilling and sustainable.

Continuing on Your Path of Personal Development and Self-Improvement

Your journey of personal development and self-improvement does not end with the completion of the

75 Day Challenge Program. Instead, consider this program as a stepping stone towards a lifelong commitment to personal growth. To continue on your path, keep these principles in mind:

Embrace a growth mindset: Cultivate a growth mindset by viewing challenges as opportunities for growth and learning, and recognizing that your abilities and skills can be developed over time.

Remain adaptable: Be open to change and willing to adapt your strategies, goals, or approaches as needed, based on your progress, feedback, and evolving circumstances.

Seek inspiration: Stay curious and open to new ideas, experiences, and perspectives, seeking inspiration from a variety of sources, such as books, podcasts, mentors, or role models.

Practice self-compassion: Be kind to yourself as you continue on your personal growth journey, recognizing that setbacks and challenges are a natural part of the process and providing yourself with the support and encouragement needed to persevere.

Celebrate your successes: Acknowledge and celebrate your achievements, both big and small, as you continue to progress towards your personal growth goals.

By embracing these principles and remaining committed to your personal development and self-improvement, you can continue to grow, learn, and thrive throughout your life.

Paying It Forward: Inspiring and Supporting Others in Their Own Personal Growth Journey

As you continue on your own path of personal growth, you have the unique opportunity to inspire and support others in their own personal growth journey. By sharing your experiences, knowledge, and insights, you can positively impact the lives of those around you and create a ripple effect of growth and development. Here are some ways to pay it forward:

Share your story: Openly share your personal growth journey with others, including both your successes and challenges, to inspire and encourage them in their own pursuits.

Offer guidance and support: Be a source of guidance and support for others, providing advice, encouragement, and resources to help them on their journey.

Create spaces for growth and learning: Organize or participate in groups, workshops, or events that foster personal growth and learning, creating a supportive environment for others to explore their own development.

Serve as a mentor or role model: Take on a mentorship role or strive to be a positive role model for others, demonstrating the benefits of personal growth and the power of perseverance.

Encourage and celebrate the success of others: Show genuine interest in the personal growth journeys of those around you, celebrating their achievements and providing encouragement during challenging times.

By paying it forward and supporting others in their personal growth journey, you not only contribute to the well-being and success of those around you but also reinforce your own commitment to personal development and self-improvement.

In conclusion, the 75 Day Challenge Program has provided a foundation for personal growth, equipping you with the skills, habits, and mindset necessary for continued development and success. As you move forward, remember to maintain the habits and lessons learned, embrace a growth mindset, and nurture supportive relationships. By staying committed to your personal growth journey and paying it forward, you can continue to evolve, inspire, and positively impact the lives of those around you.

Made in the USA
Middletown, DE
02 October 2023

39958530R00056